ज्ञानाबतार स्वामी श्रीयुक्तेश्वरेन प्रणीतम्

कैवल्यदर्शनम्

THE

HOLY SCIENCE

BY

Jnanavatar Swami Sriyukteswar Giri

ISBN: 978-1-63923-500-1

Printed: October 2022

Cover Art By: Amit Paul

Published and Distributed By:
Lushena Books
607 Country Club Drive, Unit E
Bensenville, IL 60106
www.lushenabks.com

ISBN: 978-1-63923-500-1

ज्ञानावतार स्वामी श्रीयुक्तेश्वरेन प्रणीतम्

कैवल्यदर्शनम्

THE

HOLY SCIENCE

BY

Jnanavatar Swami Sriyukteswar Giri

Jnanavatar Swami Sriyukteswar Giri

FOREWORD

Prophets of all lands and ages have succeeded in their God-quest. Entering a state of true illumination, *nirbikalpa samadhi*, these saints have realized the Supreme Reality behind all names and forms. Their wisdom and 'spiritual counsel have become the scriptures of the world. These, although outwardly differing by reason of the variegated cloaks of words, are all expressions—some open and clear, others hidden or symbolic—of the same basic truth of Spirit.

My gurudeva, Jyanavatar Swami Sri Yukteswar (1855-1936), of Serampore, was eminently fitted to discern the underlying unity between the scriptures of Christianity and *Sanatan Dharma.* Placing the holy texts on the spotless table of his mind, he was able to dissect them with the scalpel of intuitive reasoning, and to separate interpolations and wrong interpretations of scholars from the truths as originally given by the prophets.

It is due to Jyanavatar Swami Sri Yukteswar's unerring spiritual insight that it now becomes possible, through this book, to establish a fundamental harmony between the difficult Biblical chapter, *Revelation*, and the *Sankhya* philosophy of India.

As my Gurudeva has explained in his Introduction, these pages were written by him in obedience to a request made by Babaji, the holy gurudeva of Lahiri Mahasaya, who in turn was the gurudeva of Sri Yukteswar. I have written about the Christlike lives of these three great masters in my book, *Autobiography of a Yogi* (London : Rider & Co.).

The Sanskrit aphorisms cited in *The Holy Science* will shed much light on the *Bhagbad Gita* as well as on other great scriptures of India.

Paramhansa Yogananda

249 Dwapara (1949 A.D.)

INTRODUCTION.

चतुर्नवत्युत्तरशतवर्षे गते द्वापरस्य प्रयागक्षेत्रे ।
सदर्शनविज्ञानमन्वयार्थं परंगुरुराजस्याज्ञान्तुप्राप्ता ॥
कड़ारवंश्य प्रियनाथस्वामी कादम्बिनीक्षेत्रनायात्मजेन ।
हताय विश्वस्य बिदग्धतुष्णेः प्रणीतं दर्शनकैवल्यमेतत् ॥

The purpose of this book is to show as clearly as
possible that there is an essential unity in all religions ;
that there is no difference in the truths inculcated by
the various faiths ; that there is but one method by
which the world, both external and internal, has evolved;
and that there is but one Goal admitted by all scriptures. But this basic truth is one not easily comprehended. The discord existing between the different religions,
and the ignorance of men, make it almost impossible to
lift the veil and have a look at this grand verity. The
creeds foster a spirit of hostility and dissension ; ignorance widens the gulf that separates one creed from
another. Only a few specially gifted persons can rise
superior to the influence of their professed creeds and
find absolute unanimity in the truths propagated by all
great faiths.

The object of this book is to point out the harmony
underlying the various religions, and to help in binding
them together. This task is indeed a herculean one, but,
at Allahabad, I was entrusted with the mission by a holy
command. Allahabad, the sacred *Prayag-tirtha*, the
place of confluence of the Ganges, Jumna, and Saraswati
rivers, is a site for the congregation of worldly men and
of spiritual devotees at the time of *Kumbha Mela*.

Worldly men cannot transcend the mundane limit in which they have confined themselves ; nor can spiritual devotees, having once renounced the world, deign to come down and mix themselves in its turmoil. Yet men, who are wholly engrossed in earthly concerns, stand in infinite need of help and guidance from those holy beings who bring light to the race. So a place there must be where union between the two sets is possible. *Tirtha* affords such a meeting place. Situated as it is on the beach of the world, storms and buffets touch it not ; the sadhus with a message for the benefit of humanity find a *Kumbha Mela* to be an ideal place to impart instruction to those who can heed it.

A message of such a nature I was chosen to propagate when I paid a visit to the *Kumbha Mela* being held at Allahabad in January, 1894. As I was walking along the bank of the Ganges, I was summoned by a man and was afterwards honoured by an interview with a great holy person, Babaji, the gurudeva of my own guru Lahiri Mahasaya of Benares. This holy personage at the *Kumbha Mela* was thus my own Param-Guruji-Maharaj, though this was our first meeting. During my conversation with Babaji, we spoke of the particular classes of men who now frequent these places of pilgrimage. I humbly suggested that there were men greater by far in intelligence than those then present, men who were living in distant parts of the world—Europe and America —professing different creeds, and ignorant of the real significance of the *Kumbha Mela*. They were men fit to hold communion with the spiritual devotees, so far as their intelligence is concerned, yet such intellectual men in foreign lands were alas! wedded, in many cases, to rank materialism. Some of them, though famous for their investigations in the realms of science and philosophy, do not recognize the essential unity in religion. The professed creeds serve as nearly insurmountable barriers that threaten to separate mankind for ever.

My Param-Guruji-Maharaj, Babaji, smiled and, honouring me with the title of Swami, imposed on me the task of this book. I was chosen, I do not know the reason why, to remove the barrier and to help in establishing the basic truth in all religions.

The book is divided into four sections, according to the four stages in the development of knowledge. The highest aim of religion is *Atmajyanam*, Self-knowledge. But to attain this, knowledge of the external world is necessary. Therefore the first section of the book deals with वेद the gospel, and seeks to establish the fundamental truth of creation, and to describe the evolution and the involution of the world.

All creatures, from the highest to the lowest in the link of creation, are found eager to realize three things— Existence, Consciousness, and Bliss. This, the purpose or goal of all creatures, is the subject for discussion in the second section of the book. The third section deals with the method of realizing the three purposes of life. The fourth section discusses the revelations which come to those who have travelled far to realize the three ideals of life and are very near their destination.

The method I have adopted in the book is first to enunciate a proposition in Sanskrit terms of the Oriental sages, and then to explain it by reference to the holy scriptures of the West. In this way I have tried my best to show that there is no real discrepancy, much less any real conflict, between the teachings of the East and the West. Written as the book is under the inspiration of my Param-Guru-Deva, and in a Dwapara Age of rapid development in all departments of knowledge, I hope that the significance of the book will not be missed by those for whom it is meant.

A short discussion with mathematical calculation of the *Yugas* is necessary here in order to explain the fact that the present age for the world is Dwapara Yuga, and that 194 years of that *Yuga* have now (A.D. 1894) passed away, bringing a rapid development in man's knowledge.

We learn from Oriental astronomy that moons revolve around their planets, and planets turning on their axis revolve with their moons round the sun, and the sun again, with its planets and their moons, takes some star for its dual and revolves round it in about 24,000 years of our earth—a celestial phenomenon which causes the backward movement of the equinoctial points around the zodiac. The sun also has another motion by which it revolves round a grand centre called Bishnu-navi which is the seat of the creative power *Brahma*, the universal magnetism. *Brahma* regulates *Dharma* the mental virtues of the internal world. When the sun in its revolution round its dual comes to the place nearest to this grand centre the seat of *Brahma* (an event which

takes place when the autumnal equinox comes to the
first point of Aries) *Dharma* the mental virtue becomes
so much developed that man can easily comprehend all,
even the mysteries of Spirit.

DIAGRAM

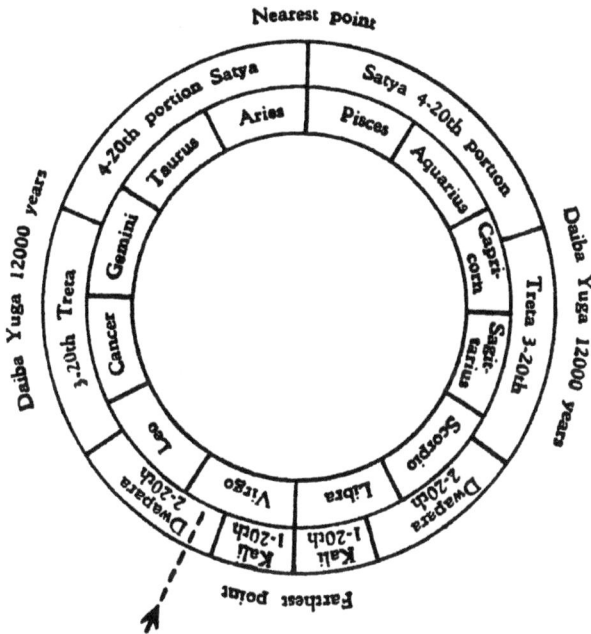

The Autumnal Equinox is now falling (at the
beginning of the twentieth century) among the fixed
stars of Virgo constellation, and in the early part
of the Ascending Dwapara Yuga.

After 12,000 years, when the sun goes to the place in its orbit which is farthest from *Brahma* the grand centre (an event which takes place when the autumnal equinox is on the first point of Libra), *Dharma*, the mental virtue, comes to such a reduced state that man cannot grasp anything beyond the gross material creation. Again, in the same manner, when the sun in its course of revolution begins to advance toward the place nearest to the grand centre, *Dharma*, the mental virtue, begins to develop ; this growth is gradually completed in another 12,000 years.

Each of these periods of 12,000 years brings about a complete change in the system, both externally in the material world, and internally in the intellectual or electric world, and is called one of the *Daiba Yugas* or Electric Couple. Thus, in a period of 24,000 years, the sun completes the revolution around its dual and finishes one electric cycle consisting of 12,000 years in an ascending arc, and 12,000 years in a descending arc.

Development of *Dharma*, the mental virtue, is but gradual and is divided into four different stages in a period of 12,000 years. The time of 1200 years during which the sun passes through 1/20th portion of its orbit (*see* Diagram) is called Kali Yuga ; *Dharma*, the mental virtue, is then in its first stage and is only a quarter developed ; the human intellect cannot comprehend anything beyond the gross material of this ever-changing creation, the external world. The period of 2400 years during which the sun passes through the 2/20th portion of its orbit is called Dwapara Yuga; *Dharma*, the mental virtue, is then in the second stage of its development and is but half complete; the human intellect can then comprehend the fine matters or electricities and their attributes which are the creating principles of this external world.

The period of 3600 years during which the sun passes through the 3/20th part of its orbit is called Treta Yuga ; Dharma, the mental virtue, is then in the third stage; the human intellect becomes able to comprehend the divine magnetism, the source of all electrical forces on which the creation depends for its existence. The period of 4800 years during which the sun passes through the remaining 4/20th portion of its orbit on either side of the point nearest the grand centre is called Satya Yuga ; Dharma, the mental virtue, is then in its fourth stage and completes its full development ; the human intellect can comprehend all, even God the Spirit beyond this visible world.

Manu, a great rishi of Satya Yuga., describes in his Samhita these Yugas more clearly in the following slokas :

"चत्वार्य्याहुः सहस्राणि वर्षाणिन्तु कृतं मुगं ।
तस्य तावच्छतीसन्ध्या सन्ध्यांशश्च तथाविघः ॥
इतरेषु ससन्ध्यासु ससन्ध्यांशेषु च तिषु ।
एकापायेन वर्त्तन्ते सहस्राणि शतानि च ॥
यदेनत् परिसंस्यातमादावेव चतुर्युगं ।
एतद्द्वादशसाहस्रं देवानां युगमुच्यते ॥
दैविकानां युगानान्तु सहस्रं परिसंख्यया ।
ब्राह्ममेकमहज्ञेयं तावती रात्रिरेव च ॥"

The period of Satya Yuga is 4000 years in duration ; 400 years before and after Satya Yuga proper are its *sandhis* or periods of mutation with the preceding and the succeeding yugas respectively; hence 4800 years in all is the proper age of Satya Yuga. In the calculation of the period of other *Yugas* and *Yuga-Sandhis*, it is laid down that numerical one should be deducted from the numbers of both thousands and hundreds which indicated the periods of the previous *Yugas* and *Sandhis*. From this rule it appears that 3000 years is the length of Treta Yuga, and 300 years before and after are its *Sandhis* the period of mutation, which make a total of 3600 years.

So 2000 years is the age of Dwapara Yuga, with 200 years before and after as its *sandhis*; a total of 2400 years. Lastly, 1000 years is the length of Kali Yuga, with 100 years before and after as its *sandhis* ; a total of 1200 years. Thus 12,000 years, the sum total of all periods of these four yugas, is the length of one of the *Daiba Yugas* or Electric Couple, two of which, *i.e.*, 24,000 years, make the electric cycle complete. 100,000 of such *Daiba Yugas* is the Day of Brahma, the Creative Power or Creator, when creation exists in a manifested state ; the period equal to the above is its night when this creative power sleeps and the creation is dissolved.

From April 11, 501 B. C. when the autumnal equinox was on the first point of Aries, the sun began to move away from the point of its orbit nearest to the grand centre toward the point farthest from it, and accordingly the intellectual power of man began to diminish. During the 4800 years which the sun took to pass through one of the Satya couples or 4/20th part of its orbit, the intellect of man lost altogether the power of grasping the spiritual knowledge. During the 3600 years following, which the sun took to pass through the descending Treta Yuga, the intellect gradually lost all power of grasping the knowledge of divine magnetism. During the 2400 years next following, while the sun passed through descending Dwapara Yuga, the human intellect lost its power of grasping the knowledge of electricities and their attributes. In 1200 more years, during the year A. D. 499, the sun had passed through the descending Kali Yuga and had reached the point in its orbit which is farthest from the grand centre; the autumnal equinox was on the first point of Libra. The intellectual power of man was so much diminished that it could no longer comprehend anything beyond the gross material of creation. The period around A. D. 500 was thus the darkest part of Kali Yuga and of the whole cycle of 24,000 years. History indeed bears out the accuracy of these ancient calculations of the Indian rishis, and records the widespread ignorance and suffering in all nations at that period.

From A. D. 499 onwards, the sun began to advance toward the grand centre, and the intellect of man started gradually to develop. During 1100 years of the Ascending Kali Yuga, which brings us to A. D. 1599, the human intellect was so dense that it could not comprehend the electricities, *Sukshmabhuta*, the fine matters of creation. In the political world, also, generally speakirtg there was no peace in any kingdom.

Subsequent to this period, when the 100-year transitional *sandhi* of Kali Yuga set in, to effect a union with the following Dwapara Yuga, men began to notice the existence of fine matters, the attributes of five electricities, *Panchatunmatra* ; and political peace began to be established.

About A. D. 1600, William Gilbert discovered magnetic forces, and observed the presence of electricity in all material substances. In 1609 Kepler discovered important laws of astronomy, and Galileo produced a telescope. In 1621 Drebbel of Holland invented the' microscope. About 1670 Newton discovered the law of gravitation. Thomas Savery made use of a steam engine in raising water about 1700. Twenty years later Stephen Gray discovered the action of electricity on the human body.

In the political world, people began to have respect for themselves, and civilization advanced in many ways. England united with Scotland became a powerful kingdom. Nepoleon Bonaparte introduced his new legal code into southern Europe. America won its independence, and Europe was peaceful in many parts. With the advance of science, the world began to be covered with railways and telegraphic wires. By the help of steam engines, electric machines, and many other instruments, fine matters were brought into practical use, although their nature was not clearly understood.

After 1899, on the completion of the period of 200 years of *Dwapara Sandhi*, the time of mutation, the true Dwapara Yuga of 2000 years will commence and will give to mankind in general a thorough understanding of the electrical attributes.

Such is the great influence of Time which governs the universe. No man can overcome. this influence except he who, blessed with pure love, the heavenly gift of nature, becomes divine ; being baptised in the sacred stream *Pranava* (the holy *Aum* vibration), he comprehends the kingdom of God.

The position of the world in the *Dwapara Sandhi* era at present (A. D. 1894) is not correctly shown in the Hindu almanacs. The astronomers and astrologers who calculate the almanacs have been guided by wrong annotations of certain Sanskrit scholars (such as Kullu Bhatta) of the dark age of Kali Yuga, and now maintain that the length of Kali Yuga is 432,000 years, of which 4994 have (in A. D. 1894) passed away, leaving 427,006 years still remaining. A dark prospect ! and fortunately one not true. The mistake crept into the almanac for the first time about 700 B. C., during the time of Raja Parikshita, just after the completion of the last Descending Dwapara Yuga. At that time Maharaja Judhisthir, noticing the appearance of the dark Kali Yuga, made over his throne to his grandson the said Raja Parikshita. Maharaja Judhisthir, together with all the wise men of his court, retired to the Himalaya Mountains, the paradise of the world. Thus there was none in the

court af Raja Parikshita who could understand the
principle of correctly calculating the ages ?of the several
yugas. Hence, after the completion of the 2400 years
of the then-current Dwapara Yuga, no one dared to
make the introduction of the dark Kali Yuga more
manifest by beginning to calculate from its first year
and to put an end to the number of Dwapara years.
According to this wrong method of calculation, therefore, the first year of Kali Yuga was numbered 2401
along with the age of Dwapara Yuga. In A. D. 499,
when 1200 years, the length of the true Kali Yuga was
complete, and the sun had reached the point of its orbit
farthest from the grand centre (when the autumnal
equinox was on the first point of Libra in the heavens),
the age of Kali in its darkest period was then numbered
by 3600 years instead of by 1200.

With the commencement of the Ascending Kali Yuga,
after A. D. 499, the sun began to advance in its orbit
nearer to the grand centre, and accordingly the intellectual power of man started to develop. Therefore
the mistake in the almanacs began to be noticed by
the wise men of the time, who found that the calculations of the ancient rishis had fixed the period of
one Kali Yuga at 1200 years only. But as the intellect of these wise men was not yet suitably developed,
they could make out only the mistake itself, and not
the reason for it. By way of reconciliation, they
fancied that 1200 years, the real age of Kali, were
not the ordinary years of our earth, but were so many
Daiba years consisting of 12 Daiba months of 30 Daiba

days each, with each *Daiba* day being equal to one
ordinary solar year of our earth. Hence according
to these men 1200 years of Kali Yuga must be equal
to 432,000 years of our earth.

In coming to a right conclusion, however, we should
take into · consideration the position of the vernal
equinox at spring in the year 1893.

The astronomical reference books show the equinox
now to be 20° 54′ 36″ distant from the first point of
Aries (the fixed star Revati), and by calculation it
will appear that 1394 years have passed away since
the time when the vernal equinox began to recede
from the first point of Aries.

Deducting 1200 years (the length of the last Ascending Kali Yuga) from 1394 years, we get 194 to indicate the present year of the world's entrance into
the Ascending Dwapara Yuga. The mistake of older
almanacs will thus be clearly explained when we add
3600 years to this period of 1394 years, and get 4994
years—which according to the prevailing mistaken
theory now represents the present year (A. D. 1894)
in the Hindu almanacs.

(Referring to the Diagram given in this book, the
reader will see that the Autumnal Equinox is now
(A. D. 1894) falling among the stars of the Virgo
constellation, and in the Ascending Dwapara Yuga.)

In this book certain truths such as those about
the properties of magnetism, its auras, different sorts
of electricities, etc., have been mentioned although

modern science has not yet fully discovered them. As for the five sorts of electricity, it may be observed here that they can be easily understood if one will direct his attention to the nerve properties which are purely electrical in nature. Each of the five sensory nerves has its characteristic and unique function to perform. The optic nerve carries light and does not perform the functions of the auditory and other nerves ; the auditory nerve in its turn carries sound only without performing the functions of any other nerves, and so on. Thus it is clear that there are five sorts of electricity, corresponding to the five properties of cosmic electricity.

So far as magnetic properties are concerned, it may be remembered that the grasping power of the human intellect is at present so limited that it would be quite useless to attempt to make the matter understood by the general public. The intellect of men in Treta Yuga will comprehend the attributes of divine magnetism (the next Treta Yuga will start in A. D. 4099). There are indeed exceptional personages now living who, having overcome the influence of time, can grasp today what ordinary people cannot grasp ; but this book is not for those exalted ones, who require nothing of it.

In concluding this introduction, we may observe that the different planets, exercising their influence over the various days of the week, have lent their names to their respective days ; similarly, the different constellations of stars, having influence over various months, have lent their names to the Hindu months. Each of the great Yugas also has much influence over the period of time covered by it; hence, in designating the years it is desirable that such terms should indicate to which Yuga they belong.

As the Yugas are calculated from the position of the equinox, the method of numbering the years in reference to their respective Yuga is based on a scientific principle; its use will obviate much inconvenience which has arisen in the past owing to the various eras being associated with persons of eminence rather than with celestial phenomena of the fixed stars. We, therefore, propose to name and number the year in which this introduction has been written as 194 Dwapara, instead of A. D. 1894, to show the exact time of the Yuga now passing. This method of calculation was prevalent in India till the reign of Raja Vikramaditya, when the *Sambat* era was introduced. As the Yuga method of calculation recommends itself to reason, we follow it, and recommend that it be followed by the public in general.

Now, in this 194th year of Dwapara Yuga, the dark age of Kali having long passed away, the world is reaching out for spiritual knowledge, and men require loving help one from the other. The publishing of this book, requested from me by my holy Param-Guru Maharaj, will, I hope, be of spiritual service.

SWAMI SRIYUKTESWAR GIRI

Serampore, Bengal.
The 26th *Falgun*, 194 *Dwapara*.
(A. D. 1894)
2

कैवल्यदर्शनम्

CHAPTER I

वेदः THE GOSPEL

नित्यं पूर्णमनाद्यनन्तंवृह्यपरसं
तदेवैकमेवाद्वैतं सत् ॥ १ ॥

The Eternal Father God *Swami Parambrahma* is the
only Real Substance, *Sat,* and is all in all in the
universe.

Man possesses eternal faith and believes intuitively
in the existence of a substance, of which
the objects of sense—sound, touch, sight,
taste, and smell, the component parts
of this visible world—are but properties. As man
identifies himself with his material body composed
of the aforesaid properties he is able to comprehend
by his imperfect organs these properties only and not
the substance to which these properties belong. The
Eternal Father God, the only substance in the universe
is, therefore, not comprehensible by man of this material
world, unless he becomes divine by lifting his self
above this creation of Darkness *Maya* Vide Hebrew
XI. 1. and John VIII. 28.

*Why God is
not compre-
hensible.*

*"Now faith is the substance of things hoped for, the
evidence of things not seen."*

"Then said Jesus unto them, When ye have lifted up the Son of man, then shall ye know that I am He———."

तत् सर्ब्बज्ञप्रेमबीजमिचत्

सर्ब्बशक्ति बीजमानन्दश्च ॥ १ ॥

2. The Almighty Force *Shakti* or in other words, the Eternal Joy *Ananda* which produces the world, and the Omniscient Feeling *Chit* which makes this world conscious, demonstrate the Nature *Prakriti* of God the Father.

'Prakriti' the Nature.

As man is the likeness of God, directing his attention inwards he can comprehend within him the said Force and Feeling, the sole properties of his self :—the Force Almighty as his will *Basana* with enjoyment *Bhoga*, and the Feeling Omniscient as his Consciousness *Chetana* that enjoys *Bhokta*. Vide Genesis I. 27.

How comprehended.

"So God created man in his own image, in the image of God created he him ; male and female created he them."

तच्छर्ब्बशक्तिर्दीजजड़प्रकृतिबासनायाः व्यक्तभावः

प्रएवशब्दः दिक्कालानबोऽपि तस्य रूपाः ॥ ३ ॥

3. The manifestation of Omnipotent Force (Repulsion, in its complementary portion Omniscient Feeling or Love the Attraction) is vibration which appears as a peculiar sound, the Word Amen *Aum*. In its different aspects Aum presents the idea of change, which is Time *Kal*, in the Ever-unchangeable ; and the idea

The word, "Amen," "Aum," is the beginning of the Creation.

of division, which is Space *Desh*, in the Ever-indivisible.

The Four Aspects. The word, time, space, and atom. The ensuing effect is the idea of particles —the innumerable atoms *patra* or *anu*. These four, viz., the Word, Time, Space and Atom, therefore, are one and the same, and substantially nothing but mere ideas.

This manifestation the Word, becoming Flesh the external material, created this visible world. So this Word Amen *Aum*, being the manifestation of the Eternal Nature of the Almighty Father or His Own Self, is inseparable from and nothing but God Himself ; as the Burning Power · is inseparable from and nothing but the Fire itself. Vide Rev. III. 14 and John I. 1, 3, 14.

"*These things saith the Amen, the faithful and true witness, the beginning of the Creation of God*"

"*In the beginning was the Word, and the Word was with God, and the word was God—all things were made by Him ; and without Him was not anything made that was made—and the Word was made flesh and dwelt among us.*"

नदेब जगत्कारएमाया ईस्वरस्य,

तस्य व्यष्टिरविद्या ॥ ४ ॥

4. These Atoms, which represent within and without the four ideas mentioned above, are the Thrones

Atoms the throne of the Creator. of Spirit the Creator that shining on them creates this universe. They are called en-masse *Maya* the Darkness, as they keep the Spiritual Light out of comprehension ; and each of them separately is called *Abidya* the Ignorance, as it makes man ignorant even of his own self. Hence the aforesaid four ideas which give rise to all those cofusions are mentioned in the Bible as so many beasts. Man, so long as he identifies himself with his gross material body, holds a position far inferior to that of the Primal four fold Atoms and necessarily fails to coprehend the same. But when he raises himself to the level thereof he not only comprehends 'this Atom both inside and outside, but also the whole creation, both unmanifested and manifested (i. e., "before and behind"). Vide Rev. IV. 6.

"And in the midst of the throne, and round about the throne, were four beasts full of eyes before and behind."

तच्छब्दब्रह्मप्रेमबीजं परा, तदेव कूटस्थचैतन्यः
पुरुषोत्तमः, तस्याभासः पुरुषः तस्मादभेदः ॥ ५ ॥

5. The manifestation of *Prembijam* Chit Attraction the Omniscient Love, is Life the Omnipresent Holy Spirit and is called the Holy Ghost *Kutastha Chaitanya* or *Purushottama* which shines on Darkness *Maya* to attract every portion of it towards Divinity. But the Darkness *Maya* or its individual parts *Abidya* the Ignorance being repulsion itself cannot receive or comprehend the Spiritual Light but reflects it. This Holy Ghost being the manifestation of the Omniscient

Kutastha-
Chaitanya the
Holy Ghost
Purushottama

Nature of the Eternal Father God is no other subs-
Avas-Chai- tance than God Himself ; and so these
tanya or reflections of Spiritual rays are called
Purush the
sons of God the Sons of God *Avaschaitanya* or *Purush*.
Vide John I. 4, 5, 11.

"In Him was Life ; and the Life was the Light of men."

"And the Light shineth in Darkness ; and the Darkness comprehended it not."

"He came unto his own, and his own received him not."

चिच्छकाशादनोमेंहृत्त्वंतन्मित्वम्, तत् सदध्यवसाय

सत्व: बुद्धि:, ततस्तद्विपरीतं मन: च रमेऽभिमानोऽ-

हंकारस्यदेव जीव: ॥ ६ ॥

6. This Atom *Abidya* the Ignorance being under the influence of Universal Love *Chit* the Holy Spirit becomes spiritualised like iron filings in magnetic
Chittwa the aura, and possessed of consciousness the
Heart. power of feeling, when it is called *Mahot*
the Heart *Chittwa*, and being such the idea of separate
Ego, Ahamkar, existence of self appears in it, which is
the Son of called *Ahamkar* Ego the son of Man.
Man. Thus being magnetized it gets two poles ;
one of which attracts it towards the Real Substance
Buddhi, the *Sat*, and the other repels it from the
Intelligence. same. The former is called *Sattwa* or
Buddhi the Intelligence which determines what is truth ; and the latter, which being a particle of Repulsion, the Almighty Force spiritualised as aforesaid, produces

the ideal world for enjoyment *ananda,* and is called

Manas, the Mind

Anandatwa or *Manas* the Mind.

तदहंकाराचित्तबिकारपेञ्चतन्त्रानि ॥ ७ ॥

तान्येब कारएशरीर: पुरूषस्य ॥ ८ ॥

तेषां तिगुणेभ्य: पञ्चदशबिषयेन्द्रियानि ॥ ९ ॥

एतानि मनोबुद्धिभ्यां सह सप्तदशसूक्ष्माङ्गानि

लिङ्गशरीरस्व ॥ १० ॥

7-10 This spritualised Atom *Chittwa* the Heart being the Repulsion manifested produces five sorts of aura—electricities—from its five different parts : one from the middle, two from the two extremities, and the other two from the spaces intervening between the middle and each of the extremities. These five sorts of electricities being

Pancha-Tattwa the Root Causes of creation is the Causal body.

attracted under the influence of Universal Love the Holy Ghost towards the Real Substance *Sat* produce a magnetic field which is called the body of *Sattwa Buddhi* the Intelligence. These five electricities being the causes of all other creations are called *Pancha-Tattwa* the five Root-causes and are named as Causal body of *Purush* the Son of God.

These Electricities being evolved from the polarised

Three Gunas the electric attributes

Chittwa are also in a polarised state and are endowed with its three attributes or *Gunas—Sattwa* the positive, *Tama* the negative, and *Rajas* the neutralising.

The positive attributes of these five electricities are the organs of sense—organs of smell, taste, sight, touch, and hearing—and being attracted under the influence of *manas* Mind the opposite pole of this Spiritualised Atom constitutes a body of the same. The neutralising attributes of them are *Karmendriyas* the organs of action—those of excretion, generation, motion, absorption, and articulation. These organs being the manifestation of the neutralising energy of the Spiritualised Atom *Chittwa* the Heart constitutes an energetic body called the body of energy the life *Pran.* And their negative attributes are the five Tanmatras or objects of the senses of smell, taste, sight, touch, and sound which, through the neutralising power of the organs of action being united with the organs of sense, satiate the desires of the Heart.

Jnyanendriyas
Jnyanendriyas the five organs of sense

Karmendriyas the five organs of action.

Bishaya or Tanmatras the five objects of Senses

These fifteen attributes with two poles—Mind and Intelligence—of the spiritualised Atom constitute *Lingasharir* or *Sukshma-sharir* the fine material body of *Purush* the son of God.

Linga-Sharir, the fine material body.

तत पञ्चतत्वानां स्यितिशीलतामसिक बिषयपञ्चतन्मात्रानां
पञ्चिवकरणेन स्युलशरीरस्याङ्गानि जड़ीभूतपञ्चक्षिल्यपृतेज-
मरुह्योमान्युद्भुतानि ॥ ११ ॥
एतान्येब चतुर्बिशतितत्वामि: ॥ १२ ॥

11-12. The aforesaid five objects, which are the negative attributes of the five electricities, being combined together produce the idea of the gross matters which appear to us in five different varieties, viz., *Kshiti* the Solid, *Ap* the Liquid, *Tej* the fiery, *Marut* the gaseous, Gross material and *Byoma* or *Akasha* the Ethereal ; these body. constitute the outer covering called *Sthulsharir* the gross material body of *Purush* the son of God.

These five gross matters and the aforesaid fifteen attributes together with *Manas* the Mind, *Buddhi* the Twenty four Intelligence, *Chittwa* the Heart, and Elders. *Ahamkar* the Ego, constitute the twenty-four principles or Elders as mentioned in the Bible. Vide Rev. IV. 4.

"And round about the throne were four and twenty seats ; and upon the seats I saw four and twenty Elders."

The aforesaid twenty-four principles which completed the creation of Darkness *Maya* are nothing but mere development of Ignorance *Abidya* ; and this Ignorance being composed only of ideas as mentioned above, this creation has no substantial existence in reality but is a mere play of ideas on the Eternal Substance God the Father.

ततूँ ब चतुर्दंशभुबनानिब्यास्ख्यातानि ॥ १३ ॥

13. This universe thus described commencing from
Seven Spheres the Eternal Substance God down to the
or Swargas. gross material creation has been distingui-
shed into seven different spheres, *Swargas or Lokas.*

(a) The foremost of these is *Satyaloka* the sphere of
7th Sphere God the only Real Substance *Sat* in the
Satayaloka. universe. No name can describe it, nor
can anything in the creation of Darkness or Light
designate it.

This sphere is therefore called *Anam* the Nameless.

(b) The next in order is *Tapaloka* the sphere of the
6th Sphere Holy Spirit which is the Eternal Patience
Tapaloka. as it remains for ever undisturbed by any
limited idea ; and because it is not approachable even by
the Sons of God as such it is called. *Agam* the Inacces-
sible.

(c) Next is *Janaloka* the sphere of spiritual reflection,
5th sphere the sons of God, wherein the idea of
Janaloka. separate existence of Self originates. As
this sphere is above the comprehension of anybody in
the creation of Darkness *Maya,* it is called *Alakshya* the
Incomprehensible.

(d) Then comes *Maharloka,* the sphere of Atom, the
4th Sphere beginning of the creation of Darkness
Maharloka. *Maya* upon which the Spirit is reflected.
This, the connecting link, is the only way between the
spiritual and material creation and is called the Door
Dasamadwar.

(e) Around this Atom is *Sivaloka* the sphere of
3rd Sphere Sivaloka. magnetic aura, the electricities. This
sphere, being characterised by the absence
of all the creation, even the organs and their objects the
fine material things, is called *Mahashunya* the great
Vacuum.

(f) The next is *Bhubaloka* the electric attributes. As
2nd Sphere Bhubaloka. the gross matters of the creation are
entirely absent from this sphere, and it is
conspicuous by the presence of the fine matters only, it
is called *Shunya* the vacuum ordinary.

(g) The last and lowest sphere is *Bhuloka* the sphere
1st Sphere Bhuloka. of gross material creation, which is always
visible to everybody.

As God created man in his own image, so is the body
Sapta Patals or seven churches. of man like unto the image of this universe. The material body of man has
also seven vital places within it called
Patals. Man, turning towards his self and advancing in
the right way, perceives the Spiritual Light in these
places which are described in the Bible as so many
Churches ; the Lights like stars perceived therein are as
so many Angels. Vide Rev. I. 12, 13, 16, 20.

"*And being turned, I saw seven golden candlesticks.—And
in the midst of the seven candlesticks one like unto the Son
of man.*"

"*And he had in his right hand seven stars.*"

"*The seven stars are the angels of the seven churches;
and the seven candlesticks which thou sawest are the seven
churches.*"

The above-mentioned Seven Spheres or *Swargas* and

Fourteen
Bhubans the
stages of
creation.

seven Patals constitute the Fourteen
Bhubans the fourteen distinguishable stages
of the creation.

तान्येब पञ्चकोषाणि पुरूषस्य ॥ १४ ॥

14. This *Purush* the Son of God is screened by five

Five Koshas or
Sheaths.

coverings called *Koshas* Sheaths.

I. The first of these five is Heart *Chittwa* the Atom

Heart the 1st.
Kosha.

composed of four ideas, as mentioned
before, which feels or enjoys and thus
being the seat of enjoyment *ananda* is called Anandamoya
Kosha.

II. The second is the magnetic aura electricities,

Buddhi the
2nd Kosha.

manifestations of Buddhi the intelligence
which determines what is truth. Thus
being the seat of knowledge *jnyan*, it is called *Jnyanamoya*
Kosha.

III. The third is the body of *Manas* the Mind, com-

"Manas" the
3rd Kosha.

posed of the organs of sense as mentioned
above, and is called the *Manamaya Kosha.*

IV. The fourth is the body of energy, life force or "Pran" the 4th Kosha. *Pran*, composed of the organs of action as described before, and so is called the *Pranamaya kosha.*

V. The fifth and the last of these sheaths is the Gross-matters the 5th Kosha. gross matter, the Atom's outer coating, which becoming *Anna* the nourishment supports this visible world, and thus is called the *Annamoya Kosha.*

The action of Repulsion the manifestation of the Action of Love. Omnipotent Energy being thus completed, the action of Attraction (the manifestation of the Omniscient Love in the core of the heart) begins to be manifested. Under the influence of this Omniscient Love the attraction, the Atoms being attracted towards one another come nearer and nearer, taking Innanimate Kingdom, Ethereal, Gaseous, Fiery, Liquid, and Solid forms. Thus this visible world becomes adorned with suns, planets, and moons which we call the inanimate kingdom of the creation.

In this manner when the action of the Divine Love Vegetable Kingdom. becomes well developed, the evolution of *Avidya* Ignorance (the particle of Darkness *Maya* the Omnipotent Energy manifested) begins to be withdrawn. *Annamoya Kosha* the Atom's outer coating of gross matter being thus with-drawn, *Pranamaya Kosha* (the sheath composed of *Karmendriya* the organs of action) begin to operate. In this organic state the

Atoms embracing each other more close to their heart appears to us as the vegetable kingdom in the creation.

When the *Pranamaya Kosha* becomes withdrawn, the Manamaya Kosha (the sheath composed **Animal Kingdom** of *Jnyanendriyas* the organs of sense) comes to the light. The Atoms then perceive the nature of the external world and, attracting other atoms of different nature, form bodies as necessary for enjoyment, and thus the animal Kingdom appears in the creation.

When *Manamaya Kosha* becomes withdrawn, *Jnyana-maya Kosha* (the body of Intelligence **Mankind** composed of electricities) becomes perceptible. The Atom, getting the power of determining right and wrong, becomes man the rational being in the creation.

When man cultivating the Divine Spirit, Omniscient Love, within his heart can withdraw this **Devata or Angel.** *Jnyanamaya Kosha*, then the innermost sheath *Chittwa* the Heart (composed of four ideas) becomes manifested. Man is then called *Debata* or Angel in the creation.

When the Heart or innermost sheath is also withdrawn, there is no longer anything **Free Sannyasi** to keep man in bondage to this creation of Darkness *Maya*. He then becomes free, *Sannyasi* the son of God, and enters into the creation of Light.

स्थुलज्ञानक्रमात् सूक्ष्मबिषयेन्द्रि यज्ञानं स्वप्नवत् ॥ १५ ॥

तत्क्रमात् मनोबुद्धिज्ञानञ्चायतथिति परीक्ष: ॥ १६ ॥

15-16. When man compares his ideas relating to
Sleeping and gross matters conceived in the wakeful
waking states state, with his conception of ideas in
dream, the similarity existing between them naturally
leads him to conclude this external world also is not
what it appears to be. When he looks for further
explanation he finds that all his wakeful conceptions
are substantially nothing but mere ideas caused by
the union of five objects of sense—the negative attributes of the five internal electricities—with the five
organs of sense their positive attributes—through the
medium of five organs of action—the neutralizing
attributes of the electricities. This union is effected
by the operation of Mind *Manas* and conceived by the
Intelligence *Buddhi.* Thus it is clear that all conceptions which man forms in his wakeful state are mere
inferential *Parokshajnyan*—a matter of inference only.

तत: सद्गुरूलाभ: भक्तियोगश्च तेन।परोक्ष: ॥ १७ ॥

17. In this way, when man understands by his
When man *Parokshajnyan* the nothingness of the ex-
gets Sat Guru ternal world, he appreciates the position
the Preceptor. of John, the Divine personage who wit-
nessed Light and bore testimony of Christ after his
heart's love, the heavenly gift of Nature, had become

developed. Any advanced sincere seeker may be fortunate in having the Godlike company of some one of such personages who may kindly stand to him as his Spiritual Preceptor, *Sat Guru*, the Saviour. Following affectionately the holy precepts of these divine personages, man becomes able to direct all his organs inward to their common centre—Sensorium, *Trikuti* or *Sushumnadwar*, the door of the interior—where he comprehends the voice, like a peculiar knocking sound the Word Amen, *Aum*, and the God-sent luminous body of *Radha*, called John in the Bible. Vide Rev. III, 13, 20. John I. 6,8,23.

Radha or John.

"*These things saith the Amen, the faithful and true witness, the beginning of the creation of God.*"

"*Behold, I stand at the door, and knock ; if any man hear my voice and open the door, I will come into him and will sup with him, and he with me.*"

"*There was a man sent from God, whose name was John.*"

"*He was not that Light, but was sent to bear witness of that Light.*"

"*He said, I am the voice of one crying in the wilderness, Make Straight the way of the Lord, as said the prophet Esaias.*"

3

From the peculiar nature of this sound, issuing as
Ganga, Jumna   it does like a stream from a higher
or Jordan the   unknown region and losing itself in the
holy Stream.   gross material creation, it is figuratively
styled by various sects of people by the names of
different rivers which they consider as sacred ; e. g.,
Ganga by the Aryans, Jumna by the Baishnava, Jordon
by the Christians, etc.

Through his luminous body, man, believing in the
The 2nd birth   existence of the true Light—the Life of
   this universe—becomes baptised or
absorbed in the holy stream of the sound. This baptism
is, so to speak, the second birth of man and is called
Bhakti yoga, without which man can never become
able to comprehend the real position of the internal
world, the kingdom of God. Vide, John I. 9, and III. 3.

"That was the true Light, which lighteth every man that
cometh into the world."

"Verily, verily I say unto thee, Except a man be born
again, he cannot see the kingdom of God."

In this state the Son of man begins to repent (Lat.
Aparoksha   repens, to creep) and turning back from
Jnyan the real   the gross material creation creeps to-
comprehen-   ward his Divinity, the Eternal Substance,
sion.   God. When the development of Ignorance begins to

recede, man gradually comprehends the true character
of this creation of Darkness, *Maya*, as a mere ideal play
of the Supreme Nature on his own self, the only
Real Substance. This true comprehension is called
Aparokshajnyan.

यदात्मानं परमात्मनि दर्शनन्ततः कैवल्यम् ॥ १८ ॥

18. When all the developments of Ignorance are
Sannyasi or
Christ the
anointed
Saviour.
withdrawn, the Heart being perfectly
clear and purified no longer merely
reflects the Spiritual Light but receives
or manifests the same, and thus being consecrated and
anointed becomes *Sannyasi* or Christ the Saviour. Vide
John I. 33.

'*Upon whom thou shalt see the Spirit descending, and
remaining on him, the same is he which baptiseth with the
Holy Ghost.*"

Through this Saviour, the Son of man becomes again
Christ or
Sannyasi the
Son of God.
baptised or absorbed in the stream of
Spiritual Light and coming above the
creation of Darkness *Maya*, enters into
the spiritual world and becomes unified with *Abhas
Chaitanya* or *Purush*, the Son of God, as was the case
with Lord Jesus of Nazareth. This is the state when
man is saved for ever and ever from the bondage of
Darkness *Maya*. Vide John I. 12 and III. 5.

"But as many as received him, to them gave he power to become the sons of God, even to them that believe on his name."

"Verily, verily, I say unto thee, Except a man be born of water and of the Spirit, he cannot enter into the kingdom of God."

When man, thus entering into the spiritual world, **Sacrifice of self.** becomes a Son of God, he comprehends the universal Light—the Holy Ghost— as a perfect whole, and his self as nothing but a mere idea resting on a fragment of the *Aum* Light. Then he sacrifices himself to the Holy Ghost the altar of God, i. e., abandons the vain idea of his separate existence and becomes one integral whole. Thus being one with the universal Holy Spirit of God the Father, **Kaivalya the unification.** he becomes unified with the Real Substance, God. This unification of self with the Eternal substance God, is called *Kaivalya*, Vide Rev. III. 21.

"To him that overcometh will I grant to sit with me in my throne, even as I also overcame, and am set down with my Father in his throne."

CHAPTER II

अभीष्ट: । THE GOAL

अत: मुक्तिजिज्ञासा ॥ १ ॥

1. When man understands even by way of inference
Liberation the prime object. the true nature of this creation, the true relation existing between that creation and himself, when he further understands that he is completely blinded by the influence of Darkness, *Maya,* and that it is the bondage of Darkness alone which makes him forget his real self and brings about all his sufferings, he naturally wishes to be relieved from all these evils. This relief from evil, or the liberation from the bondage of Darkness, *Maya,* becomes the prime object of his life.

मुक्तिस्वरूपेऽबस्थानम् ॥ २ ॥

2. When man raises himself above the ideal creation
Residing in self Liberation. of this Darkness, *Maya,* and passes completely out of its influence, he becomes liberated from bondage and is placed in his real self the Eternal Spirit.

तदा सर्व्वक्लेशनिबृत्ति: परमार्थसिद्धिश्च ॥ ३ ॥

3. On attaining this liberation, man becomes saved
Liberation is   from all his troubles, and all the desires
Salvation.   of his heart are fulfilled, so the ultimate
aim of his life is accomplished.

इतरत्र कामापूर्णो जन्मजन्मान्तरव्यापी

क्लेशमयदु:खम् ॥ ४ ॥

4. So long, however, as man identifies himself
Why man   with his material body and fails to find
suffers.   repose in his true self, he feels his wants
according as his hearts desires remain unsatisfied.
To satisfy them he has to appear often in flesh and
blood on the stage of life, subject to the influence
of Darkness, Maya, and has to suffer all the troubles
of life and death not only in the present but in the
future as well.

क्लेशमविद्यामातृम् ॥ ५ ॥

भावेऽभावोऽभावेभाव इत्येवस्वोधमविद्या ॥ ६ ॥

5-6. Ignorance, Abidya, is misconception, or is the
What is   erroneous conception of the existence of
Ignorance ?   that which does not exist. Through

abidya man believes that this material creation is the only thing which substantially exists, there being nothing beyond; forgetting that this material creation is substantially nothing and is a mere play of ideas on the Eternal Spirit, the only Real Substance beyond the comprehension of the material creation. This ignorance is not only a trouble in itself but is also the source of all other troubles of man.

तदेबाब रएविंज्ञेपशक्तिविशिष्टत्वात् क्षेतृमस्मिताभिनिबेश-
राग‌द्वेषानाम् ॥ ७ ॥

तस्याब रएशक्तै रस्मितैभिनिबेशी
बिक्षेपशक्तेश्च रागद्वैषौ ॥ ८ ॥

स्वामिशक्तोरबिबिक्त ज्ञानमम्मिता ॥ ९ ॥

प्राकृतिकसंस्कारमातृमभिनिबेशः ॥ १० ॥

सुखकरबिषयतृष्एा रागः ॥ ११ ॥

दुःखकरविषयत्यागतृष्णाद्वेषः ॥ १२ ॥

7-12. In order to understand how this Ignorance is

Ignorance is the Source of all troubles. the source of all other troubles we should remember (as has been explained in the previous chapter) that Ignorance, *Abidya*, is nothing but a particle of Darkness, *Maya*, taken distributively, and as such it possesses the two properties of *maya*. The one is its darkening power by the influence of which man is prevented from grasping anything beyond the material creation. This darkening power produces *Asmita* or *Egoism* being the identification

of self with the material body which is but the development of Atom, the particles of the universal force ; and
Avinibesha or Tenacity to the Condition. By virtue of
the second of the properties of *Maya*, Ignorance or *abidya*
in its polarised state produces an attraction for certain
objects and repulsion for others. The objects so attracted are the objects of pleasure for which an Attachment,
Raga, is formed. The objects that are repulsed are the
objects producing pain for which an Aversion, *Dwesha*,
is formed.

क्लेशमूल कम्मंत द्विपाक एव दु:ख: ॥ १३ ॥

13. By the influence of these five troubles, viz.,
Ignorance, Egotism, Attachment, Aver-
sion, and Tenacity to the material crea-
tion, man is induced to involve himself in egoistic works
and in consequence he suffers.

Why man works.

सर्वदु:खानां निवृतिरित्यार्थ ॥ १४ ॥

निवृत्येपनुवृत्यभाब: परम: ॥ १५ ॥

14-15. With man the cessation of all sufferings is
Artha, the heart's immediate aim. The
complete extirpation of all these suffer-

Ultimate aim of the heart.

ings, their recurrence becoming impossible, is the *Para-martha*, the ultimate goal.

सर्व्वंकामपूर्णत्वे सर्व्बंदु:खमूलक्लेशनिवृति:
तदा परमार्थ सिद्धि: ॥ १६ ॥

सन्चिदानन्दमयत्त्वप्राप्तिरिति तियकामा: ॥ १७ ॥

सद्गुरूदत्तसाघनप्रभावात् चित्तस्य प्रसाद:
एवानन्द: ॥ १८ ॥

तत: सर्व्बं दु:खानां हानन्तदा
सर्व्वंभाबोदयश्चित ॥ १९ ॥

तत: ग्रात्मनो नित्यत्वोपलब्धि: सत् ॥ २० ॥

तदेव स्वरूप: पु पस्य ॥ २१ ॥

16-21. Man naturally feels great necessity for *Sat*
Existence, *Chit* Consciousness, and
Ananda Bliss. These three are the real
necessities of the human heart and have nothing to do
with anything outside his self. They are essential properties of his own nature, as explained in the previous
chapter.

The real necessities.

When man becomes fortunate in securing the favour
of any divine personage *Satguru* the
Saviour, and affectionately following his
holy precepts is able to direct all his organs inward, he
becomes capable of satisfying all the wants of his heart
and can thereby get contentment, *Ananda*, the Real
Bliss.

How man gets Bliss

With his heart thus contented, man becomes able to fix his attention upon anything he chooses and can comprehend all its aspects. So *Chit* Consciousness of all the modifications of Nature up to its first and primal manifestation the Word Amen *Aum*, and even of his own Real Self, gradually appears. And being absorbed in the stream thereof, man becomes baptised and begins to repent towards his Divinity the Eternal Father, whence he had fallen. *Vide* Revelation II, 51.

How Consciousness appears.

"*Remember therefore from whence thou art fallen, and repent.*"

Man, being conscious of his own real position and of the nature of this creation of Darkness *Maya*, becomes possessed of absolute power over it, and gradually withdraws all ·the developments of Ignorance. In this way, coming above the control of this creation of Darkness *Maya*, he comprehends his own self as Indestructible and Ever-existing Real Substance. So *Sat* the Existence of Self comes to light.

How Existence is realised.

All the necessities of the heart—viz., *Sat* Existence, *Chit* Consciousness, and *Ananda* Bliss— having been attained, Ignorance the mother of evils becomes emaciated ; and consequently all troubles of this material

How the main object of the heart is attained.

world, which are the sources of all sorts of sufferings, cease for ever. Thus the ultimate aim of the heart is affected.

तदा सर्ब्बकामपूर्णोपरमार्थसिद्धिकात्
गुणानाम्प्रतिप्रसवे आत्मनः स्वरूप
प्रतिष्टा तदेब कैबल्यम् ॥ २२ ॥

22. In this state, all the necessities having been
How Man gets
Salvation.
attained and the ultimate aim effected, the heart becomes perfectly purified and instead of reflecting the spiritual light receives the same ; and thus being consecrated or anointed by the Holy Spirit, becomes Christ the anointed, Saviour. Entering the kingdom of Spiritual Light, becomes the Son of God.

In this state man comprehends his Self as a fragment of the Universal Holy Spirit, and abandoning the vain idea of his separate existence unifies himself with the Eternal Spirit, i.e., becomes one and the same with God and Father. This unification of Self with God is *Kaivalya* which is the Ultimate Object of the created Being. Vide John XIV, 11.

"*Believe me that I am in the Father, and the Father in me.*"

CHAPTER III

साधन। THE PROCEDURE

तप: स्वाध्यायब्रह्मनिधानानि यज्ञ: ॥ १ ॥

मात्रास्पर्शेषु तितिज्ञा तप: । २ ॥

आत्मतत्त्वापदेशश्चबसममननिधिध्यासंनमेव

स्वाध्याय: ॥ ३ ॥

प्र एबशब्द एव पन्था ब्रह्मन: तस्मिन्

आत्मसमर्पणं ब्रह्मनिधानम् ॥ ४ ॥

1-4 *Tapa* is religious mortification or Patience

Patience Faith and Holy works explained

both in enjoyments and sufferings. *Shadhyaya is Shraban*, study, with *manan*, the attention and there by *Nidhidhyasan*; forming of an idea of the true Faith about Self *i.e.,* what I am, whence I came, where shall I go, what I have come for, and such other matters concerning Self. *Brahmanidhan* is the Baptism or merging of self in the stream of the Holy Sound, *Pranava*, which

is the holy Work to attain salvation and the only way
by which man can repent to his Divinity the Eternal
Father, whence he had fallen. Vide Rev. II. 19.

"*I know thy works, and charity, and service, and faith, and
thy patience and thy works ; and the last to be more than the
first.*"

श्रद्धावीर्य्यस्मृतिनममाध्यानुष्ठानात्

तस्याविभविः ॥ ५ ॥

स्वभाबजप्रेमस्य बेगतीव्रताश्रद्धा ॥ ६ ॥

5-6, This Holy Sound *Pranova* *Sabda* appears
spontaneously through culture of *Sradd-*
ha the energetic tendency of heart's
natural love, *Veerya* the moral courage,
Smiriti the true conception and *Samadhi* the true concentration.

This heart's natural love is the principal thing, to
attain a holy life.   When this love the
heavenly gift of nature appears in the
heart, it removes all exciting causes from
the system and cools it down to a perfectly normal
state, and envigorating the vital powers excretes all

*How the Holy
Sound appears*

*The virtue of
Love*

foreign matters—the germs of diseases—from it by natural ways, perspiration, etc., and thereby makes man perfectly healthy, in body and mind, and enables him to understand the proper guidance of nature. When this love becomes developed in man, it makes him able to understand the real position of his own self as well as of other surrounding him. With the help of this developed love, man becomes fortunate in gettig the Godlike company of the divine personages and is saved for ever. Without this love man cannot live in the natural way, neither can he keep company of the fit person for his own welfare ; he becomes often excited by the foreign matters taken into his system through mistakes in understanding the guidance of nature, and in conse-quence he suffers in body and mind. He can never get any peace whatever and his life becomes a burden. Hence the culture of this love the heavenly gift is the principle thing for the attainment of holy salvation ; it is beyond doubt impossible for man to advance a step towards the same without it. Vide Rev. II. 2-4.

"I know thy works, and thy labour, and thy patience, and how thou canst not bear them which are evil : and thou hast tried them which say they are apostles, and are not, and hast found them liars.

"And hast borne, and hast patience, and for my name's sake hast laboured, and hast not fainted.

*"Nevertheless I have some what against thee, because thou
hast left thy first love."*

शुद्धासेवित सद्गुरो: स्वभाबजोपदशपालने

वीर्य्यलाभ: ॥ ७ ॥

सब्वें एब गुरुव: सन्तापहा‍रक: संशयछेदक:

शान्तिप्रदायक:

सत् तत्सङ्ग ब्रह्म बत्‍करनीयं, विपरीतमसत्

बिपबढ़ज्जनीयम् ॥ ८ ॥

7-8. As explained in the previous chapter, this
creation is substantially nothing but a mere ideal play
of Nature on the only Real Substance God the Eternal
Father who is Guru—the Supreme—in this universe.
All things of this creation are therefore no other substance than this Guru, the Supreme Father God Himself,
perceived in plurality by the manifold aspects of the play
of nature. Vide John X, 34, and Psalms LXXXII, 6.

*"Jesus answered them, Is it not written in your law,
I said, Ye are gods ?*

*"I have said, ye are gods ; and all of you are children of
the most High."*

Out of this creation, and object which relieves us of our miseries and doubts, and administers peace to us, however insignificant the same may be, whether animate or inanimate, is entitled to our utmost respect, Even it be an object of vilest contempt for others, it should be accepted as Saviour *sat* and its company as godlike which should always be kept. That which produces the opposite results of destroying our peace, throwing us into doubts, and creating our miseries, should be considered *Asat* the bane of all good and should be avoided as such. This idea led the Indian sages to say—

"*Apshu deva manushyanam dibideva manishinam kash-thaloshtrashu murkhanam Juktashyatman devata.*"

Man to get salvation choose as their Saviour the objects which they can comprehend according to their own acquirements. Thus in general, people would think that illness is a dire calamity, and as water, when properly administered, tends to remove illness they may choose for their Saviour or Divinity water itself. Philosophers, being able to comprehend the internal electric light which shines within them, find their heart's love flow energetically towards the light that relieves them of all exciting causes, cools down their systems to a normal state, and envigorating their vital powers, makes them perfectly healthy, both in body and in mind. They then accept this light as their Divinity or the Saviour. Ignorant people in their blind faith would accept a piece of wood or stone as their Saviour or Divinity in the external creation for which their heart's natural love will develop till by its energetic tendency it will relieve them of all exciting causes in their system and cool their system down to a normal state and invigorate their vital powers. The adepts, on the other hand, having full control over the whole material world, find their Divinity or Saviour in Self and not outside in the external world.

To keep company with one is not only to be with his person, but also to associate him with heart's love and to be one with him in principle. This has been very well expressed by Lord Bacon : "A crowd is not a Company, it is a mere gallery of faces." To keep company, therefore, with the god like object is to associate him with *sraddha*, *i. e.*, heart's love intensified in the sense above explained, by keeping his appearances and attributes fully in mind, and by reflecting on the same and affectionately following his instructions lamblike. Vide John L 29.

How to keep Company.

"*Behold the Lamb of God, which taketh away the sin of the world.*"

By so doing, when man becomes able to conceive the sublime status of his divine brothers, he may be fortunate in remaining in their company, and in

4

securing help from any one of them whom he may choose as his Spiritual Preceptor, *Sat-Guru* the Saviour.

Thus, to resume—*veerya* or moral courage can be obtained by the culture of *Sraddha*, *i.e.*, by devoting one's natural love to his preceptor, by being always in his company, and following with affection his holy instructions as they are freely and spontaneously given.

तद्वीर्यं यमनियमानुष्ठानात् द्रढ़भूमि: ॥ ९ ॥

अहिंसासत्यास्तेयब्रह्मचर्यापरिग्रहादय यम: ॥ १० ।

शौचसन्तोषसह‌ रूपदेशपालनादय: नियम: ॥ ११ ॥

9-11. Firmness of moral courage can de attained by the culture of *yama*, the religious forbearances *i.e.*, abstention from cruelty, dishonesty, covetousness, unnatural living, and unnecessary possessions ; and by *niyama*, the religious observances, *i.e.*, purity in body and mind; cleaning the body externally and internally from all foreign matters which being fermented creates different sorts of diseases in the system, and clearing the mind from all prejudices and dogmas which make one narrow ; contentment in all circumstances ; and obedience to the holy precepts of the Divine personages.

To understand what natural living is, it will be necessary to distinguish it from what is unnatural. Living depends upon the selection of (1) Food, (2) Dwelling, and (3) Company. To live naturally, the lower animals

What is natural living ?

can select these for themselves by the help of their instinct and the natural sentinels placed at the sensory entrances, viz, the organs of sight, smell, and taste. With men in general these organs, however, are so much perverted by unnatural living from very infancy that no reliance can be placed on their judgments. To understand, therefore, what our natural needs are, we ought to depend upon observation, experiment and reason.

First, to select our natural food, our observation should be directed to the formation of the organs which aid in digestion and nutrition, viz., the teeth and digestive canal ; to the natural tendency of the organs of sense which guide animals to their food ; and to the nourishment of the young.

What is Natural Food for man ?

By observation of the teeth we find that in carnivorous animals the incisors are little developed, but the canines are of striking lengths, smooth and pointed, to seize the prey ; the molars also are pointed ; these points, however, do not meet but fit closely side by side to separate the muscular fibres. In the herbivorous animals the incisors are strikingly developed, the canines are stunted though occasionally developed into weapons as in elephants, the molars are broad-topped and furnished with enamel on the sides only. In the frugivorous all the teeth are nearly of the same height, canines are little projected, conical, and blunt

Observation of teeth.

(not intended obviously for seizing prey but for exertion of strength). The molars are broad-topped and furnished at the top with enamel folds to prevent waste caused by their side motion, but not pointed to help in chewing flesh. In omnivorous animals like bears on the other hand, the incisors resemble those of the herbivorous, the canines are like those of the carnivorous and the molars are both pointed and broad topped to serve a twofold purpose.

Now if we observe the formation of the teeth in man we find that these do not resemble those of the carnivorous, neither do they resemble the teeth either of the herbivorous or of the omnivorous. They do resemble, exactly, those of the frugivorous animals : the reasonable inference, therefore, is that man is a frugivorous or fruit-eating animal.

By our observation of the digestive canal we
Observation of the digestive canal. find that the bowels of carnivorous animals are 3 to 5 times the length of their body, measuring from the mouth to the anus ; and their stomach is almost spherical. The bowels of the herbivorous are 20 to 28 times the length of their body and their stomach is more extended and of compound build. But the bowels of the frugivorous animals are 10 to 12 times the length of their body, and their stomach is somewhat broader than that of the carnivorous and has a continuation in the duodenum serving the purpose of a second stomach. This is exactly the formation

we find in human beings, though Anatomy says that the human bowels are 3 to 5 times the length of their body—making a mistake by measuring the body from the crown to the soles, instead of from mouth to anus. Thus we can again draw our inference that man is, in all probability, a frugivorous animal.

By observation of the natural tendency of the organs Observation of the organs of sense. of sense, the guideposts to determine what is nutritious and by which all animals are directed to their food, we find that when the carnivorous animal finds a prey, he becomes so much delighted that his eyes begin to sparkle, and he boldly seizes the prey and greedily laps the jetting blood ; while, cn the contrary, the herbivorous animal refuses even his natural food, leaving it untouched, if it is sprinkled with a little blood. His senses of smell and of sight lead him ·to select grass and other herbs for his food, which he tastes most delightfully. Similarly, with the frugivorous animal, we find that their senses always direct them to fruits of the trees and field. In men also, we find that their senses of smell, etc. never lead them to slaughter any animal ; on the contrary they can not bear even the sight of it. Slaughter-houses are always recommended to be removed far from the towns ; men often pass strict ordinances forbidding the uncovered transportation of flesh meats. Can flesh then be styled as the natural food of man, when both his eyes and nose are so much against it, unless his senses are deceived by cooking with spices, salt, sugar, etc.? On the other hand, how delightful do we find the fragrance of fruits, the very sight of which even makes the mouth water. It may also be noticed that various grains and roots possess an agreeable odour and taste, though faint, even when unprepared. Thus again we are led to infer from these observations that man was decidedly intended to be a frugivorous animal.

By the observation of the nourishment of the young, **Observation of the nourishment of the young.** we find that milk is undoubtedly the food of the new-born babe. Abundant milk is not supplied in the breasts of the mother, if she does not take fruits, grains, and vegetables as her natural food.

Hence from these observations the only conclusion **Cause of Disease** that can reasonably be drawn is that various grains, fruits, roots, and—for beverage—milk, and pure water openly exposed to air and sun are decidedly the best natural food for man. These being congenial to the system when taken according to the power of the digestive organs, well chewed and mixed with saliva, are always easily assimilated. Other foods are unnatural to men and being uncongenial to the system are necessarily foreign to it. When these foods get access to the stomach, they are not properly assimilated. Mixed with the blood, they accumulate in the excretory and other organs not properly adapted to them. When they cannot find their way out, they subside, in tissue crevices by the law of gravitation, and being fermented produce diseases, mental and physical ; and ultimately lead to premature death.

Experiment also proves that the non-irritant diet
Children's Development. natural to the vegetarian is, almost without exception, admirably suited to children's development both physical and mental. Their mind, understanding, will, the principal faculties, temper and general dispositon are also properly developed. We find that when extraordinary means such as excessive fasting, scourging, or monastic confinement are resorted to for the purpose of suppressing the sexual passions, these means seldom produce the desired effect. Experiment shows however that the man can easily overcome these passions, the arch-enemy of morality, by natural living on a non-irritant diet, above referred to ; thereby they get a calmness of mind which every psychologist knows is the most favourable to mental activity and to a clear understanding as well as to a judicial way of thinking.

Something more should be said here about the
Sexual Desire. natural instinct of propagation, which is, next to the instinct of self-preservation, the strongest in the animal body. Sexual desire like all other desires has a normal and an abnormal or diseased state ; the latter resulting only from the foreign matter accumulated by unnatural living as mentioned above. In the sexual desire every one has

a very accurate thermometer to indicate the condition of his health. This desire is forced from its normal state by irritation of nerves resulting from the pressure of foreign matter accumulated in the system, which is exerted on the sexual apparatus and is at first manifested by an increased sexual desire followed by the gradual decrease of potency. This sexual desire in its normal state makes man quite free from all disturbing lusts, and operates on the organism awaking a wish for appeasement only very infrequently. Here again experiment shows that this desire like all other desires is always normal in individuals who lead a natural life as mentioned.

The sexual organ (the junction of important nerve extremities, particularly of the sympathetic

The root of the tree of life. and the spinal nerves which are the principal nerves of the abdomen, which, through their connection with the brain, are capable of enlivening the whole system) is in a sense the root of the tree of life. Man well-instructed in the proper use of sex can keep his body and mind in proper health and can live a pleasant life throughout. The practical teachings of sexual health cannot be taught because, the public regards the subject as unclean and indecent. Thus blinded, mankind presumes to clothe nature in a veil because she seems to them impure, forgetting that she is always clean and that everything impure and improper lies in man's ideas, and not in nature herself. It is clear therefore that man, not knowing the proper use of the sexual organ and being compelled to wrong practices by the nervous irritation resulting from unnatural living, suffers troublesome diseases in life and ultimately becomes a victim of premature death.

Secondly, about our dwelling place. We can easily understand, when we feel displeasure on entering our crowded rooms after breathing fresh air on a mountain top or in an expanse of field or garden, that the atmosphere of the town or any crowded place is quite an unnatural dwelling place. The fresh atmosphere of the mountain top or of the field or garden or of a dry place under trees covering a large plot of land and freely ventilated with fresh air is the proper dwelling place for man according to Nature.

Dwelling place of man.

And thirdly, as to the company we should keep. Here also, if we listen to the dictates of our conscience and consult our natural liking, we will at once find that we favour those persons whose magnetism affects us harmoniously, who cool our system, internally invigorate our vitality, develop our natural love, and thus relieve us of our miseries, and administer peace to us. This is to say, we should be in the company of the *Sat* or Saviour and should avoid that of the *Asat*, as described before. By keeping the company of *Sat* or Saviour, we are enabled to enjoy perfect health, physical and mental, and our life is prolonged ; if on the other hand we disobey the warning

Natural Company.

of Mother Nature, without listening to the dictates of our pure conscience, and keep the company of whatever has been designated as *Asat,* an opposite effect is produced and our health is impaired and our life shortened.

Thus natural living being indispensable to the practice of *Yama* the ascetic forbearance as explained above, to make any attempt to practise *Yama* without living naturally is altogether useless. Purity of mind and body being equally indispensable to the practice of *Niyama,* the ascetic observance as explained · above, every attempt should be made to attain that purity.

Necessity of Natural living and purity.

तत: पाशक्षय: ॥ १२ ॥

घृणालज्जाभयशोकजुगुप्साजातिकुलमानानि

पाशाष्टकानि ॥ १३ ॥

तदा चित्तस्य महत्वम् वीरत्वमूधा ॥ १४ ॥

गाईस्थाश्रमापयोग्यासनप्राणायामप्रत्याहार —

साधनेषु योग्यता च ॥ १५ ॥

स्थिरसुखमासनम् ॥ १६ ॥

प्राणानां संयम: प्राणायाम: ॥ १७ ॥

इन्द्रियाणामन्तर्मुखत्वम्प्रत्याहार: ॥ १८ ॥

13-18. Firmness of moral courage when attained removes all the obstacles in the way of salvation. These obstacles are of eight sorts, viz., hatred, shame, fear, grief, condemnation, race distinction, pride of pedigree, and a

Meanness of human heart.

narrow sense of respectability, which are the meannesses
of the human heart. By the removal of these obstacles,
Beeratwam or *Mahatwam* (magnanimity of
How magnani- the heart) comes in and this makes man
mity appears. fit for the practice of *Asanam* (remaining
in steady and pleasant posture), *Pranayamah* (control
over *Prana*, involuntary nerves), and *Pratyaharah*
(changing the direction of organs, the voluntary nerves,
inward.) These practices enable man to satisfy his
heart by enjoying the objects of senses and are intended
for *Garhyasthashram* (domestic) life.

Man can put the voluntary nerves into action whenever he likes and can give them rest when
Necessity of fatigued. When all of these nerves
Pranayamah. require rest he sleeps naturally and by
this sleep all these voluntary nerves, being refreshed,
can work again with full vigour. His involuntary nerves,
however, irrespective of his will, are working conti-
nuously of themselves since his birth, as he has no
control over them he cannot interfere with their action
in the least. When these nerves become fatigued they
also want rest and naturally fall asleep. This sleep of
the involuntary nerves is called *Mahanidra*, the great
sleep or death. When this takes place, the circulation,
respiration, etc., being stopped, the material body naturally begins to decay. After a while, when this great
sleep *Mahanidra* is over, man awakes with all his desires,
and finding his body unfit for further work leaves the
same and goes somewhere else to create a new one for

the accomplishment of his desires. In this way man binds himself to life and death and hence fails to get salvation.

But if man can control these involuntary nerves by the aforesaid *Pranayamah*, he can stop the natural decay of the material body and put the involuntary nerves to rest at times as is the case with his voluntary nerves. After this rest these involuntary nerves also become refreshed and work with a new life again. As, after sleep, when full rest has been taken by the voluntary nerves, no help is required to be awakened, so after death, also, when full rest has been taken by the involuntary nerves, no help is necessary to be in life again. If man can die, *i.e.*, put his entire nervous system to rest, controlling the natural decay of the body by the aforesaid *Pranayamah*, the nerves then being not much fatigued, life comes into play much sooner than after ordinary death and the whole system being refreshed begins to work with full vigour. Thus life and death come under control. In this manner man, saving his present body, from decay and from the terrible sufferings of death and requiring no further time for the necessary development of any other material body, can fulfil all the desires of his heart. Thus he is no more required to come into the world under the influence of darkness *Maya* and to suffer again a second death. Vide Rev. II 10, 11.

Control Over Death.

"*Be thou faithful unto death, and I will give thee a crown of life,*"

"*He that overcometh shall not be hurt of the second death.*"

Man enjoys a thing when he so desires. At the. time of the enjoyment, however, if he directs his organs of sense through which he enjoys, towards the object of his desire, he can never be satisfied, and his desires increase in double force. On the contrary, if he can direct his organ of sense inward toward his self at that time, he can satisfy his heart immediately. So the practice of the aforesaid *Pratyaharah*, the changing of the direction of organs—the voluntary nerves—inward, is essentially necessary for the satisfaction of the worldly desires, by which man remains bound and cannot get salvation from the creation of Darkness, Maya.

Necessity of Pratyaharah

Man cannot feel or even think properly when his mind is not in a pleasant state ; and the different parts of the human body are so harmoniously arranged that even if any minutest part of it be moved a little, the whole system becomes disturbed. So to comprehend a thing, *i.e.*, to feel a thing by the heart clearly, the practice of the aforesaid *Asanam*, the steady and pleasant posture, is extremely necessary.

Necessity of Asanam.

चित्तप्रसादे सति सर्व्वभावोदय: स्मृति: ॥ १९ ॥

तदेवार्थमात्रनिर्भासं स्वरूपशून्यमिव समाधि: ॥ २० ॥

तत: संयम: तस्मात् ब्रह्मप्रकाशक—

—प्रणवशब्दानुभव: ॥ २१ ॥

तस्मिन्नात्मनो योगो भक्तियोगस्तदा दिव्यत्वम् ॥ २२ ॥

19-22. Man, when expert in the above-mentioned practices, becomes able to conceive or feel all things of this creation by his heart. This true conception is called *Smriti*.

Smriti the conception.

Fixing attention firmly on any object thus conceived, when man becomes as much identified with the same as if he were devoid of his individual nature, he attains the state of *Samadhi* or true concentration.

Samadhi the concentration.

When man directs all his organs of sense towards their common centre the sensorium or *Sushumnadwarah* the door of the internal world, he perceives his God-sent Luminous body *Radha* or John, and hears the peculiar knocking Sound *Pranava Sabda* the word of God. Vide John I. 6, 7, 23.

Pranava Sabda, the Word of God.

"There was a man sent from God, whose name was John."

"The same came for a witness, to bear witness of the Light, that all men through him might believe."

"I am the voice of one crying in the wilderness."

Thus perceiving, man naturally believes in the

Samyamah
the concen-
tration of self

existence of the true Spiritual Light and withdrawing his self from the outer world concentrates himself on the sensorium. This concentration of the self is called *Samyamah.*

By this *Samyamah* or concentration of self to the

Bhaktiyoga
or Baptism
the second
birth of man

sensorium, man becomes baptized or absorbed in the holy stream of the Divine Sound. This baptism is called *Bhaktiyoga.* In this state man repents, *i. e.,* turning from this gross material creation of Darkness *Maya*, he creeps back towards his Divinity the Eternal Father whence he had fallen, and passing through the senssorium, the door, enters into an internal sphere *Bhuba-Loka.* This entrance into the internal world is the second birth. to man. In this state man becomes *Debata,* a Divine Being.

मूढविक्षिप्तक्षिप्तैकाग्रनिरुद्धाश्चित्तभेदास्ततः

जात्यन्तरपरिणामः ॥ २३ ॥

23. There are five states of the human, heart, viz.,

Five states of
human heart

Dark, Propelled, Steady, Devoted, and Clean. By these different states of the heart man is classified, and his evolutionary status determined.

मूढ़चितस्य विपर्य्ययवृत्ति वशाद् जीवस्य शूद्रत्वम्,

तदा ब्रह्माएः कलामात्रेन्द्रियग्राह्यस्थूलविषयं

प्रकाशात् कलिः ॥ २४ ॥

24. In the dark state of the heart man misconceives,
i. e., he thinks that this gross material
The Dark Heart portion of the creation is the only real
substance in existence and there is
nothing besides. This, however, is contary to the truth,
as has been explained before, and is nothing but the
effect of Ignorance *Abidya.* In this
Sudra or servant class state man is called *Sudra* or belonging
to the servant class ; because his natural
duty then is to serve the higher class people in order
to secure their company and thereby prepare his heart to
attain a higher stage. This state of man is called *Kali* ;
and whenever in any solar system, man
Kali-yuga the dark cycle generally remains in this state and is
ordinarily deprived of the power of
advancing beyond the same, the whole of that system
is said to be in *Kali-yuga* the dark cycle.

ब्रह्माएः प्रथमपादपूर्णे द्वितीयसूक्ष्मविषय

ज्ञानाप्राप्तसन्निकाते चित्तस्य विक्षेपस्तदा

प्रमाएवृत्ति वशात् क्षत्रियत्वम् ॥ २५ ॥

ततः सद्गुरुलाभः भक्तियोगश्च

तदा लोकान्तिरगमनम् ॥ २६ ॥

25-26. When man becomes a little enlightened he compares his experiences relating to the material creation gathered in his wakeful state with his experiences in dream, and, understanding the latter to be merely ideal, begins to entertain doubts as to the substantial existence of the former. His heart then becomes propelled to know the real nature of the universe and, struggling to clear the doubts, seeks for evidence to determine what is truth. In this state man is called *Kshattriya*, or one of the Military classes ; and to struggle in the manner aforesaid becomes his natural duty by whose performance he may get an insight into the nature of creation, and attain the real knowledge of it. This Kshattriya state of man is called *Sāndhisthal*, the place between higher and lower. In this state men, becoming anxious for real knowledge, need help of one another ; hence mutual love, the principal thing for getting salvation, appears in the heart. By the energetic tendency of this love man affectionately keeps company with those who destroy troubles, clear doubts, and afford peace to him ; and hence avoids, whatever produces the contrary result ; he also studies scriptures of the divine personages scientifically. In this way man becomes able to appreciate what true Faith is, and understands the real position of the divine personages when he may be fortunate in securing the godlike company of some one of them who may kindly stand

The Propelled Heart

Kshattriya the Military classes.

Sandhisthal— the place between higher and lower

When man gets sat guru, the saviour

5

to him as his spiritual preceptor *sat guru*, the saviour. Following affectionately the holy precepts he learns to concentrate his self, directing his organs of sense to their common centre, sensorium. *Sushumnadwar* the door of the internal sphere; where he perceives the luminous body John or *Radha*, and heard the holy sound Amen *Aum* like a stream or river, and, being absorbed or baptized in it, begins to repent (creep back) towards his Divinity the Eternal Father through the different *Lokas* the spheres of the creation.

भुर्भुव:खर्मेंहृजनस्तप:सत्येति सप्त लोका: ॥ २७ ॥

27. In the way towards Divinity there are seven spheres or stages of creation, designated as *Swargas* or *Lokas* by the oriental sages, as described in Chapter I, 16; viz., *Bhu Loka* the sphere of gross matters; *Bhuba Loka* the sphere of fine matters or electric attributes; *Swa Loka* the sphere of magnetic poles and aura or electricities; *Maha Loka* the sphere of magnet the Atom; *Jana-Loka* the sphere of spiritual Reflection the son of God; *Tapa Loka* the sphere of the Holy Ghost the Universal Spirit; and *Satya Loka* the sphere of God the Eternal substance *Sat*. Of these seven places, the first three, viz., *Bhu Loka*, *Bhuba Loka* and *Swa Loka*, comprise the material creation the kingdom of Darkness *Maya*, and the last three, viz., *Satya Loka*, *Tapa Loka* and *Jana Loka* comprise the spiritual creation the kingdom of Light. *Maha Loka* the sphere of Atom being in

The Seven Lokas

the midst is said to be the door communicating between these two the material and spiritual creation, and is called *Dasamadwar* the tenth door, or *Brahmarondhra* the way to the Divinity by the Indian sages.

भुवर्लोके ब्रह्माएः द्विवौयपादसूक्ष्मान्तजंगत्

प्रकाशात् द्वापरः जीवस्य द्विजत्वञ्च तदा

चित्तस्य क्षिप्तत्वात्तस्य वृति विकल्पः ॥ २८ ॥

28. When man being baptized begins to repent (creep back) towards the Eternal Father and, withdrawing his self from the gross material world the *Bhu Loka*, enters into the world of fine matter the *Bhuba Loka*, he is said to belong to the *Dwija* or twice-born class. In this state he comprehends his internal electricities the second fine material portion of the creation, and understands that the existence of the external is substantially nothing but mere coalescence or union of his fine internal objects of sense the negative attributes of electricities, with his five organs of sense the positive attributes, through his five organs of actions, the neutralizing attributes of the same, caused by the operation of his mind and conscience.

Dwija or Twice-Born

This state of man is *Dwapara* ; and when this becomes the general state of the higher beings naturally in any solar system, the whole of that system is said to be in *Dwapara Yuga.* In this state, the heart becomes steady.

The Steady Heart

If man continues in the baptized state, remaining immersed in the holy stream, he gradually comes to a pleasant state when his heart wholly abandons the ideas of the external world and becomes devoted to the internal one.

स्वर्गे चित्तस्यैकाग्रतया स्तस्य वृत्ति:स्मृति स्तत:
ब्रह्मएस्तृतीयपादजगत्कारए प्रकृति ज्ञानवशात्
तृ ेता तदा विप्रत्त्वं जीवस्य ॥ २९ ॥

29. In this devoted state man, withdrawing his self from *Bhuba Loka* the world of electric attributes, comes to *Swa Loka* the world of magnetic attributes, the electricities and poles ; he then becomes able to comprehend *Chitta*, heart, the magnetic third portion of the creation. This *Chitta*, as has been explained in chapter I, is the spiritualized Atom *Abidya* or Ignorance a part of Darkness *Maya*. Man, comprehending this *Chitta*, becomes able to understand the whole of Darkness *Maya* itself, of which *Chitta* is a part, as well as the entire creation. Man is then said to belong to the *Bipra* or nearly perfect class. This state of human being is called *Treta* ; when this becomes the general state of the higher being naturally in any solar system the whole of that system is said to be in *Treta Yuga*.

The Devoted Heart

(51)

महल्लोके चित्तस्य निरूब्धत्ततस्य वृत्तिनिद्रा

ततःसर्ब्बंविकाराभावे व्रह्मवस्त्वात्मानुभवात्

व्राह्म एत्वन्तदा व्रह्म एत्नुरीयांशसत्पदार्थ-

प्रकाशात् सत्यम् ॥ ३० ॥

30. Man repenting (creeping back) further lifts up
his self to *Maha Loka* the region of
The Clean magnet; then all the development of
Heart Ignorance being withdrawn the heart
comes to a clean state, void of all external ideas. Then
man becomes able to comprehend the spiritual Light
Brahma, the Real Substance in the universe, which
is the last and everlasting spiritual portion in Creation.
In this stage man is called *Brahman* or spiritual
class. This state of the human being is called *Satya*
and when this becomes the general state of the higher
beings naturally in any solar system the whole of
that system is said to be in *Satya Yuga*.

तदपि सन्यासात् मायातीतजनलोकस्थं

मुक्तः सन्यासी ततः चैतन्यप्रक्टतितपलोके

आत्मानमर्पणात् सत्यलोकस्थं कैवल्यम् ॥ ३१-३२ ॥

31-32. In this way when the heart becomes perfectly
purified it does no more reflect but receives spiritual
·Light, the Son of God, and thus being consecrated or

anointed by the Spirit it becomes Christ the Saviour. This is the only way through which man, being again baptized or absorbed in Spirit, can rise above the creation of Darkness *Maya* and enter into *Jana Loka* the Kingdom of God, *i. e.*, the creation of Light. In this state man is called *Jiban Mukta Sannyasi*, like Lord Jesus of Nazarath. Vide John III. 5, and XIV. 6.

"Verily, verily, I say unto thee, except a man be born of water and of the Spirit, he cannot enter into the kingdom of God."

"Jesus saith unto him, I am the way, the truth, and the life : no man cometh unto the Father, but by me."

32. In this state man comprehends himself as nothing but a mere ephemeral idea resting on a fragment of the universal Holy Spirit of God, the Eternal Father, and understanding the real worship he sacrifices his self there at this Holy Spirit the altar of God, i.e., abandoning the vain idea of his separate existence he becomes dissolved or dead in the universal Holy Spirit; and thus reaches *Tapa Loka* the region of Holy Ghost.

In this manner, being one and the same with the universal Holy Spirit of God, man becomes unified with the Eternal Father Himself, and so comes to *Satya Loka*, in which he comprehends that all this creation is substantially nothing but a mere ideal play of his own Nature, and that nothing in the universe·

exists besides his own Self. This state of unification is called *Kaivalya*, the only Self. Vide Rev. XIV. 13 and John XVI. 28.

"*Blessed are the dead which die in the Lord from henceforth.*"

"*I came forth from the Father ; and am come into the world : again, I leave the world, and go to the Father.*"

CHAPTER IV

विभूति—THE REVELATION

सहजद्रव्यतपोमन्त्रैभिः देहत्रयशुद्धिस्ततः सिद्धिः ॥ १ ॥

सद्गुरु कृपया तल्लभ्या ॥ २ ॥

सहजद्रव्येण स्थूलस्य तपसा सूक्ष्मस्य

मन्त्रेण कारणदेहचित्तस्य च शुद्धिः ॥ ३ ॥

1-3. Adeptship is attainable by the purification of the body in all respects. Purification of the material body can be effected by things generated along with it by Nature; that of the electric body by patience in all circumstances ; and that of the magnetic body (चित्त chitta) by the regulation of the breath which is called *mantra* (मनः त्रायते इति मन्त्रः) the purifier of the mind. The process of how purifications can be effected may be learnt at the feet of the divine personages who witness Light and bear testimony of the Christ consciousness.

साधनप्रभावेन प्रएवशब्दाविर्भाव-

स्तदेवमन्त्रचैतन्यः ॥ ४ ॥

देशभेदे तस्य भेदात् मन्त्रभेदः साधकेषु ॥ ५ ॥

4-5. By culture of regulation of the breath as directed by the spiritual preceptor *satguru,* the holy word *Pranava* or *Sabda* (प्रएाब, शब्द) appears by itself or becomes audible. When this holy word *Pranava* or *Sabda* appears, mantra the breath becomes regulated and checks the decay of the material body.

This *Pranava* appears in different forms at the different stages of advancement according to the purification of the heart *chitta.*

शुद्धायुक्तस्य मद्गरुलाभस्तत: प्रवृत्ति-
न्दैव प्रवर्तकावस्था जीवस्य ॥ ६ ॥

6. It has already been explained what *Satguru* is and how to keep the company thereof. Man when endowed with the heavenly gift of pure love naturally becomes disposed to avoid the company of what is *asat* and to keep the company of what has been described as *sat.* By affectionately keeping the company of *sat* he may be fortunate enough to please one who may kindly stand to him as his *satguru* or spiritual preceptor. By keeping his godlike company there grows an inclination *Prabritti* in the disciple's heart to save himself from the creation of darkness *Maya,* and he becomes *prabartaka* an initiate in the practices of *yama* and *niyama,* the ascetic forbearance and observance necessary to obtain salvation.

यमनियमसाधनेन पशुत्वनाशस्तत:
वीरत्वमासनादिसाधने योग्यता च
तदैव साधकावस्था प्रवर्त्तकस्य ॥ ७ ॥

7. It may be remembered that by the culture of yama and niyama the eight meannesses vanish from the human heart and magnanimity comes in. It is at this stage that man becomes fit for the practice of ascetic posture, etc., the processes pointed out by his satguru to attain salvation; when he continues to practise the processes so pointed out to him he becomes a sadhaka or disciple.

तत: भावोदयात् दिव्यत्वं तस्मिन्
समाहितंहृदिववाणी प्रएवान् भवस्तदैव
सिद्धावस्था साधकस्य ॥ ८ ॥

8. On a reference to Chapter III it will be found how a disciple, while passing through the different stages, becomes able to conceive the different objects of creation in his heart, and how he gradually advances to the state of meditation, and ultimately by concentrating his attention to the sensorium, he perceives the peculiar sound Pranava or Sabda the holy word, when the heart

becomes divine, and the *Ego, Ahankara* or the Son of Man, becomes merged or baptised in the stream thereof and the disciple becomes *siddha,* an adept a Divine personage.

In the state of baptism *bhakti yoga, surat sabda yoga,* man repents and withdraws his self from the external world of gross matters the *bhuloka,* and enters into the internal one of fine matter the *bhubarloka,* where he perceives the manifestation of spirit the true light like seven stars in seven centres or conspicuous places which have been compared to seven golden candlesticks. These stars, being the manifestation of true light the spirit, are called Angels or *Rishis* which appear one after another in the right hand of the Son of Man, i.e., in his right way to the Divinity. The seven golden candlesticks are called the seven churches, *patals,* the seven conspicuous places in the body, known as brain the *sahasrara,* medulla oblongata the *ajnya chakra,* and five other centres, *viz.,* cervical *bisuddha,* dorsal *anahata,* lumbar *manipur,* sacral *swadhisthan,* and coccygeal *muladhar,* where the Spirit becomes manifested. Through these seven centres or churches, the *ego* or Son of Man passes towards the Divinity. *Vide Rev. I. 12, 13, 16, 20 and II. I.*

"*And being turned, I saw seven golden candlesticks, And in the midst of the seven candlesticks one like unto the son of man.........And he had in his right hand seven stars:*"

"*The mystery of the seven stars which Thou sawest in my right hand, and the seven golden candlesticks.*"

*The seven stars are the angels of the seven churches ;
and the seven candlesticks which thou sawest are the
seven churches."*

*"These things saith he that holdeth the seven stars
in his right hand, who walketh in the midst of the
seven golden candlesticks."*

तत् संयमात् सप्तपातालदर्शनम्

ऋषिसप्तकस्य चाविर्भवि: ॥ ९ ॥

9. In this state of baptism *bhaktiyoga* or *surat sabda,
yoga* the Ego *surat* the son of Man, gradually passing
through the seven places mentioned above, acquires
the knowledge thereof ; and when he thus completes
the journey through the whole of these regions he
understands the true nature of the universe. Withdrawing his self from *bhubarloka* the fine material
creation, he enters into *swarloka*, the source of all
matters, fine and gross. There he perceives the luminous
astral form around his heart Atom, the throne of
Spirit the Creator, provided with five electricities and
with two poles, Mind and Intelligence, of seven different
colours as in rainbows. In this sphere of electricities,
mind, and intelligence, the source of all objects of
senses and of organs for their enjoyment, man becomes
perfectly satisfied with being in possession of all objects
of his desires, and acquires a complete knowledge
thereof. Hence the astral form aforesaid with its
electricities and poles, the seven parts thereof, has

been described as a sealed casket of knowledge, a book with seven seals. Vide Rev. V. 1 and IV. 3.

"*And I saw in the right hand of him that sat on the throne a book written within and on the backside sealed with seven seals.*"

"*And there was a rainbow round about the throne.*"

तदा ज्ञानशक्तियोगकृमात्
मण्म्स्वर्गीधिकार स्नतइचतुर्मणुनामाविर्मिव: ॥ १० ॥

10. Passing through this *swarloka*, the son of Man comes to *maharloka*, the place of magnet of which the ideas of manifestation, time, space, and particle (or atom) are the four component parts. As has been already mentioned in Chapter I, this *maharloka* represents *Abidya*, the Ignorance, which produces the idea of separate existence of self, and is the source of Ego the Son of Man. Thus man *manava* (मानव) being the offspring of Ignorance, and the Ignorance being represented by the four ideas aforesaid, these Ideas are called the four *Manus* (मनु+ष्ण =मानव) the origins or sources of man.

नन: भूतज्ञयादणिमाचैश्वर्यस्याविर्मिव: ॥ ११ ॥

11. The *maharloka* the place of magnet as explained before is the *Brahmarandhra* or *dasamdwara* the door

between two creations material and spiritual. When Ego the Son of Man comes to the door he comprehends the spiritual light and becomes baptised therein. And passing through this door he comes above the ideal creation of Darkness *Maya*, and, entering into the spiritual world, receives the true Light and becomes the Son of God. Thus man being the Son of God overcomes all bondage of darkness *Maya* and becomes possessed of all *aisharyyas*, the ascetic majesties. These *aisharyyas* are of eight sorts, *viz* :—

1. *Anima*, the power of making one's body or anything else as small as he likes even as an atom *anu*.

2. *Mahima*, the power of magnifying or making one's body or anything else *mahat* as large as he likes.

3. *Laghima*, the power of making ones body or anything else *laghu* as light as he likes.

4. *Garima*, the power of making ones body. or anything else *guru* as heavy as he likes.

5. *Prapti*, the power of *apti*, obtaining anything he likes.

6. *Basitwa*, the power of *basha*, *i.e.*, bringing anything under control.

7. *Prakamya*, the power of satisfying all desires *Kama* by irresistible will force.

8. *Ishitwa*, the power of becoming *isha* Lord over everything. Vide John XIV, 12.

"Verily, verily, I say unto you, He that believeth on me, the works that I do shall he do also ; and greater works than these shall he do ; because I go unto my Father."

तत: सृष्टिस्थितिप्रलयज्ञानात् सर्व्वनिवृत्तिः ।
तदा मायातिक्रान्ते आत्मानं परमात्मनि
दर्शनात् कैवल्यम् ॥ १२ ॥

12. Thus man being possessed of *aishaṛyas* the ascetic majesties aforesaid fully comprehends the Eternal Spirit the Father, the only Real Substance, as Unit, the Perfect Whole, and his self as nothing but a mere idea resting on a fragment of the Spiritual Light thereof. Man, thus comprehending, abandons altogether the vain idea of the separate existence of his own self and becomes unified with him the eternal Spirit, God the Father. This unification with God is *Kaivalya* the ultimate object of this treatise. Vide Rev. III 21.

"To him that overcometh will I grant to sit with me in my throne, even as I also overcame, and am set down with my Father in his throne."

CONCLUSION

" Love rules the court, the camp, the grove,
The men below and saints above ;
For love is heaven and heaven is love."

The power of love has been beautifully described by the poet in the stanza quoted above. It has been clearly demonstrated in the foregoing pages that "Love is God," not merely as the noblest sentiment of a poet but as an aphorism containing an eternal truth. To whatever religious creed a man may belong and whatever may be his position in society, if he properly cultivates this ruling principle naturally implanted in his heart, he is sure to be on the right path, to save himself from this creation of Darkness *Maya*. It has been shown in the foregoing pages how love may be cultivated, how by its culture it attains development, and when developed how, through this means only, man may find his spiritual preceptor, through whose favour he again becomes baptized in the holy stream, and sacrifices his self before the altar of God, becoming unified with the Eternal Father for ever and ever. This little volume is therefore concluded with an earnest exhortation to the reader that he may never forget that life is always unsafe and unstable, like a drop of water on a lotus leaf, and that the company of a Divine personage even for a moment can save it, like Noahs ark in the flood. This thought

has been very poetically described by the Indian sage
Shankaracharya in the following slokas—

"नलिनीदलगतजलमति तरलम्
तद्वज्जीवनमतिशयचपलम् ।
क्षणमिह सज्जनसङ्गतिरेका
भवति भवार्णवेतरणे नौका ॥"

THE END